JUN 1 7 2015

DATE DUE

MAY 2 3 2016			
			PRINTED IN U.S.A.

THE LIFE CYCLE OF A
BUTTERFLY
By Robin Merritt

The Child's World

Published by The Child's World®
1980 Lookout Drive
Mankato, MN 56003-1705
800-599-READ
www.childsworld.com

The Child's World®: Mary Berendes, Publishing Director
The Design Lab: Kathleen Petelinsek, design
Red Line Editorial: Editorial direction

ISBN: 978-1-60973-143-4
LCCN: 2011927699

Printed in the United States of America
Mankato, MN
July 2011
PA02089

CONTENTS

Life Cycles...4

What Is a Butterfly?...7

A Butterfly's Body...8

An Egg Hatches...12

Eating and Growing...15

Big Changes...19

Out Comes a Butterfly...20

A Female Lays Eggs...27

The Life Cycle Continues...28

Life Cycle Diagram...30

Web Sites and Books...32

Glossary...32

Index...32

LIFE CYCLES

Every living thing has a life cycle. A life cycle is the steps a living thing goes through as it grows and changes. Humans have a life cycle. Animals have a life cycle. Plants have a life cycle, too.

A cycle is something that happens over and over again. A life cycle begins with the start of a new life. It continues as a plant or creature grows. And it keeps going as one living thing creates another, or **reproduces**—and the cycle starts over again.

A butterfly's life cycle has four main steps: egg, **larva**, **pupa**, and adult butterfly.

At each step in a butterfly's life cycle, the insect looks very different.

A cabbage white butterfly has white wings with black spots.

WHAT IS A BUTTERFLY?

Butterflies are insects, like ants and flies. They have four wings like moths. But moths come out at night, while butterflies usually fly in the day.

There may be more than 15,000 different kinds of butterflies fluttering all over the world. They can be many different colors. Some look plain like white petals, and some have stunning colors and patterns. The black and orange monarch butterfly is one of the most common butterflies in North America.

A BUTTERFLY'S BODY

Like all insects, a butterfly has three main body parts. One of these is the head. On it are two feelers, or **antennae**. A butterfly uses these to smell for food.

A butterfly's mouthparts look like a long, coiled straw. The tube uncoils to sip up food. For most butterflies, this is the sweet nectar found in flower blooms. The tube rolls up again when the insect has had its fill.

A butterfly's long, tube-like mouthparts coil up when not in use.

A butterfly breathes through tiny holes in its **thorax** and **abdomen**.

The middle part of a butterfly's body is the thorax. Six legs and four delicate wings grow from this part. Taste sensors on the end of each leg allow butterflies to taste with their feet. Thousands of scales cover each wing. The scales give the wings colors and patterns.

The back part of a butterfly's body is called the abdomen. Inside the abdomen are the butterfly's heart and many other organs. The abdomen and thorax also have holes that let air inside so the butterfly can breathe. A tough covering protects all three parts of a butterfly's soft body.

AN EGG HATCHES

Every species of butterfly goes through a set of changes called **metamorphosis**. The butterfly grows a lot as it changes from egg to larva to pupa to adult. But each species of butterfly is unique. The life cycle of a monarch butterfly begins inside a tiny, white egg. The egg sticks to the leaf of a milkweed plant. In about four days, a larva **hatches**. It chomps through its eggshell and crawls out of the egg.

Ants, wasps, and other insects eat monarch butterfly eggs.

A butterfly larva is also called a caterpillar.

EATING AND GROWING

The monarch larva is hungry! Unlike an adult, the larva has strong jaws that can chew and chew. The first thing a larva eats is its own eggshell. Then the larva starts eating milkweed leaves. The new larva eats as much as it can. Eating milkweed makes the caterpillars taste bad, so many **predators** do not eat monarch caterpillars.

The larva's body grows very quickly, but its skin cannot stretch as it grows. Soon its body gets too big for its skin. The old skin splits and the larva wriggles out. Its new skin is bigger than its old skin. The larva will shed its skin, or **molt**, about five times as it grows. Each time it looks a little different. But the last time it molts is the most exciting.

A larva goes through a few steps to molt. Its tight, old skin breaks open. Then the larva wriggles out and leaves the old skin behind.

In its final molt, the larva becomes a pupa.

BIG CHANGES

After about two weeks, the butterfly larva finally stops eating. It is ready to enter a new step in its life cycle. It finds a safe place under a leaf or a branch. Then it spins a pad of silky threads and clings to it upside down. Then the larva molts one last time.

But this time there is a tough case around the larva instead of a new skin. The tough case protects the larva while big changes happen inside. The larva's body is breaking down. It has become a pupa, or **chrysalis**. Inside, butterfly wings and other body parts are forming.

OUT COMES A BUTTERFLY

About ten days later, the case splits. A crumpled-looking adult butterfly pushes out and hangs upside down. Fluid pumps into its wings, and they unfold. As the wings spread out and dry, their full colors show. In monarch butterflies, males and females have somewhat different wing patterns. The butterfly rests and warms in the sun for a while. Then, it flies away.

A butterfly can fly a few hours after leaving its tough case.

Birds, frogs, and spiders are butterfly predators.

In spring and summer, monarchs fly from flower to flower looking for sweet nectar. They also fly to escape birds or other predators. Luckily, monarch adults taste bad from their caterpillar diet of milkweeds.

A butterfly's main job is to find a mate and reproduce. If a female smells a mate with her antennae, she flies toward him. When they mate, the female's eggs are **fertilized** inside her body. Fertilized eggs can become new butterflies.

Most monarch butterflies live for about two to six weeks. Some monarchs hatch late in the summer. They can live up to eight months. As winter approaches, these special monarchs begin a journey as long as 2,500 miles (4,023 km).

These monarchs travel part of the way in big groups. They fill the skies with their fluttering orange wings. They flap and flap to warmer climates in Southern California or Mexico. There, thousands of monarchs gather in trees. In spring, they mate. As they fly north, females search for milkweed.

Large groups of monarch butterflies travel to warm places for the winter. They gather in trees.

The female monarch lays her eggs in a safe place.

A FEMALE LAYS EGGS

A female monarch tastes a leaf with her feet to make sure it is milkweed. Milkweed is the only food the larva will eat when it hatches.

The butterfly lays a single egg on the underside of a leaf. Then she moves on to another leaf and lays another egg. She might lay 100 or more eggs, but only a few of these will hatch. Most of the eggs are eaten by predators or destroyed by rain or wind.

THE LIFE CYCLE CONTINUES

Inside the egg, an **embryo** grows. Soon, it will be a larva ready to eat its way out of its egg and crawl into a bright, spring day. The life cycle of the butterfly continues.

After a larva hatches from the egg, it will look for food so it can grow.

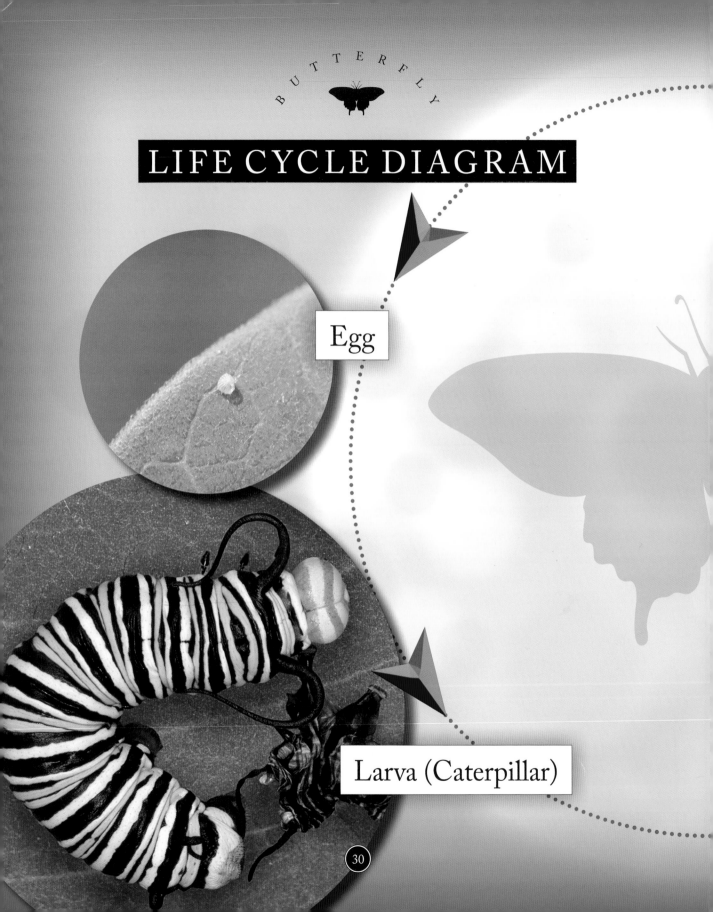

LIFE CYCLE DIAGRAM

Egg

Larva (Caterpillar)

Adult Butterfly

Pupa (Chrysalis)

Books

Bishop, Nic. *Butterflies and Moths*. New York: Scholastic Nonfiction, 2009.

Frost, Helen, and Leonid Gore. *Monarch and Milkweed*. New York: Atheneum Books for Young Readers, 2008.

Murawski, Darlyne. *Face to Face with Butterflies*. Washington, DC: National Geographic, 2010.

Glossary

abdomen (AB-duh-muhn): The abdomen is the rear section of an insect's body. A butterfly's heart and many other organs are inside its abdomen.

antennae (an-TEN-ee): Antennae are thin feelers on an insect's head. Butterflies use their antennae for smelling.

chrysalis (KRISS-uh-liss): A chrysalis is an insect in the life cycle stage between larva and adult. A butterfly chrysalis is also called a pupa.

embryo (EM-bree-oh): An embryo is an organism in the early stages of growth. A butterfly embryo grows inside an egg.

fertilized (FUR-tuh-lyzd): Fertilized refers to an egg that can grow and develop into a new life. When butterflies mate, eggs are fertilized inside the female's body.

hatches (HACH-ez): When something hatches, it breaks out of an egg. A monarch egg hatches after about four days.

larva (LAR-vuh): A larva is an animal soon after hatching that looks very different from its parents. A butterfly larva is also called a caterpillar.

metamorphosis (met-uh-MOR-fuh-siss): Metamorphosis is the series of changes some animals go through between hatching and adulthood. Butterflies go through metamorphosis.

molt (molt): To molt is to shed old skin and grow new skin. A butterfly larva will molt about five times as it grows.

predators (PRED-uh-turs): Predators are animals that hunt and eat other animals. Some birds are butterfly predators.

pupa (PYOO-puh): A pupa is an insect in the life cycle stage between larva and adult. A butterfly pupa is also called a chrysalis.

reproduces (ree-pruh-DOOS-ez): If an animal or plant reproduces, it produces offspring. A butterfly reproduces when it lays eggs that hatch and grow into new butterflies.

thorax (THOR-aks): A thorax is the middle section of an insect's body. Wings and legs grow from a butterfly's thorax.

Index

abdomen, 11
antennae, 8, 23

breathing, 11

caterpillar, 15, 23
chrysalis, 19

egg, 4, 12, 15, 23, 27–28
embryo, 28

flowers, 8, 23
flying, 7, 20, 23, 24

hatching, 12, 24, 27, 28
head, 8

insects, 7, 8

jaws, 15

larva, 4, 12, 15–16, 19, 27, 28
laying eggs, 27
legs, 11
life span, 24

metamorphosis, 12
milkweed, 12, 15, 23, 24, 27
molting, 16, 19
monarch butterfly, 7, 12, 15–16, 19–20, 23–24, 27–28
moths, 7
mouthparts, 8

nectar, 8, 23

organs, 11

predators, 15, 23, 27
pupa, 4, 12, 19

reproduce, 4, 23, 24

thorax, 11

wings, 7, 11, 19, 20, 24